MW00699609

I AM MY

Mother's

DAUGHTER

I AM MY Mother's DAUGHTER

The Purpose, The Pain & The Shame

Rev. Dr. Nellie Taylor-Walthrust

ZizaCreative
PUBLISHING, INC.

I Am My Mother's Daughter
The Purpose, The Pain & the Shame

Copyright © 2015 by Nellie Walthrust

Requests for information should be directed to:
ZizaCreative Publishing, Inc.
718.708.3348
New York

Cover & Interior Design by ZizaCreative Publishing, Inc.
Cover Photograph © Sezer Alcinkaya

Printed in the United States of America

ISBN-10: 0-692-58789-6
ISBN-13: 978-0-692-58789-8

All scriptures are from the New International Version
and the New Living Translation of the Bible.

THIS BOOK IS DEDICATED TO
the memory of my mother, Olivia Taylor Marrow Daniels;
a woman like no other. She gave me life, nurtured me, taught me,
held me, kissed me, but most importantly loved me unconditionally.

She left fingerprints of grace on my life. There are not enough words
I can say to describe how important my mother was to me,
and what a powerful influence she continues to be.
Her legacy will never be forgotten.

FROM A MOTHER'S HEART

*"I will instruct you and teach you in the way you should go;
I will counsel you and watch over you." Psalm 32:8*

*"I will praise God's name in song and glorify
Him with thanksgiving." Psalm 69:30*

I Love You Mama

table
OF CONTENTS

FOREWORD

Have you ever asked, *"Why me?"* The question *"Why?"* is universal to the human experience. *"Why* did I (or someone I care about) have to endure painful, heartbreaking circumstances?"

In the case of this book, *what purpose* could there be for a shy young girl named Nellie – already coping with the harsh consequences of the segregated South – to bear the additional agonies of feeling unwanted, suffering verbal abuse, experiencing grief at a tender age, and struggling with low self-esteem?

In II Corinthians 1:3-4 the Apostle Paul writes, *"(v.3) Praise be to the God and Father of our Lord Jesus Christ, the Father of compassion and the God of all comfort, (v.4) who comforts us in all our troubles, so that we can comfort those in any trouble with the comfort we ourselves receive from God."*

For over 18 years, it has been my privilege to work alongside the Rev. Dr. Nellie Taylor-Walthrust. Now that I know her story as recorded in these pages, I can make some of the "compassion connections" between God's comfort in her young life and the consolation she unselfishly offers to others in her various roles.

As an ordained minister in our church, "Rev. Nellie" (as we affectionately call her) serves with distinction. Whether she is proclaiming God's Word publicly, or ministering privately at the altar to a hurting soul, or putting together a fellowship event, "Rev. Nellie" can be counted on to do everything with a smile and with the enthusiasm that exudes the love of God. She has a servant's heart.

But don't mistake her gentleness for cowardice. She courageously advocates for the vulnerable and needy and confronts societal evils through her faith in God. As the Director of the Leeds Place of the North Shore Child and Family Guidance Center, Rev. Dr. Nellie Taylor-Walthrust takes her compassion outside the church walls into the community. Given her past, it is also providential that Dr. Walthrust has taken a leading role in promoting the health of pregnant moms and their babies through the "Good Beginnings for Babies" initiative. I have also proudly observed her successful leadership role in the large "National Night Out" events she has helped organize year after year in the Westbury/New Cassel Community.

Rev. Nellie is the same Christ-honoring person, whether she is sharing the stage with a government official or encouraging a child during a youth service. On an even more personal note, my wife Elizabeth and I consider Rev. Nellie and her husband, Deacon Elliott Walthrust, great friends, true encouragers and important role models in both family and ministry life.

As you read these pages, may the LORD's comforting and equipping work in Rev. Nellie inspire you to trust Him for your present and your future as well.

REV. STEPHEN SAMUEL, M. DIV., SENIOR PASTOR
Westbury Gospel Tabernacle | Long Island, New York

A WORD FROM THE AUTHOR

It has been nearly eight years since I attempted to write this book. Years ago, while attending a Mother's Day service at my church, I listened as Pastor Beverly Caesar, who was the guest speaker for the service, shared her story about being an unwanted child. Her parents had gone to a local doctor in her native country of Jamaica, West Indies to have her aborted. She spoke about the doctor, when he entered the examining room, how he immediately said to her mother, "I cannot touch you because there is a powerful light around you." Her parents left the clinic, not knowing what else to do. They were afraid, but a few months later, their baby girl was born. God had a plan that later in her life she would fulfill His purpose of doing a great work for the Lord Jesus Christ.

It was affirmed to me, after hearing her story, that the Lord had a purpose for my life as well. It was alright to put aside 50 years of guilt and shame so that I could share with others what He had brought me through.

Years went by, and it was almost daily that I created this book in my heart and head, but not on paper. However, the closer I came to writing down my thoughts, the more excuses I would make. So for several reasons, I gave up telling what was in my heart.

LISTENING TO MY FEARS

Every time I thought about the catastrophic events that took place in my childhood, I relived the pain. Whenever I pondered those moments and the moments afterward, it seemed like they happened yesterday, and I was still that little girl nobody wanted. My day would end with my heart filled with sadness and self-pity. So, my desire to write stopped. My attitude became apathetic, and I pushed the book to the side.

But every time I pushed it aside, something or someone would always remind me of the task that I was avoiding. I needed to follow the leading of the Holy Spirit, who had directed me to write in the beginning. It was as if the voice in my head was saying, *"Move forward, you can do this."* But, the pain in my heart said, *"Leave it alone because it hurts too much; forget it -- your story can't help anyone."* It was a tug of war going on between my head and my heart, and I wasn't sure which one was winning.

I attempted to ignore the voice, but the more I ignored it, the louder the voice became. I began telling myself every excuse I could think of. I criticized my thought patterns and the way I wrote. I nearly convinced myself that what I had to say wouldn't be a source of strength to anyone. I feared that what I had to say was not a part of my purpose. I was afraid of revealing the pain, the shame, and my insecurities.

HEARING FROM THE LORD

One Sunday evening in March 2013, as I was preparing to minister at the evening service at my church, the Lord had given me a word to share. For several weeks prior to the service, the Lord had been speaking to me almost daily about hearing the voice of God and responding immediately. I knew exactly what He was saying to me. I realized that His timing is not my timing, and there was a task that He wanted me to respond to right away.

Once again, all the questions, doubts, and fears began to plague my mind, but this was a pivotal moment in my life. The voice in my head was saying, *"For we walk by faith and not by sight."* II Corinthians 5:7. My entire life has been a walk of faith. Early in life, as a small child, I placed my faith and confidence in God that one day the hopes and dreams He had placed in my heart would come to pass. I never doubted His love for me. The first song I learned as a child became my anthem, *Yes, Jesus Loves Me.* I related this song to my life's experiences. When those around me who were supposed to show love did not, I always found comfort in singing this little song. I truly believed then, and now I know, that Jesus loves me.

Even though I was afraid, I was tired of not doing what, deep in my heart, I knew God had called me to do. I reminded myself of II Timothy 1:7, *"For God has not given us a spirit of fear, but of power, of love, and of a sound mind."* Instead of focusing on the negatives, I focused on the fact that God was about to utilize my pain and my shame to fulfill His purpose in my life. With a willing heart and a testimony of God's faithfulness, love, and restoration, I began to understand the pain that God allowed me to endure.

TRUSTING THE LORD

Today I understand that every heartache carries a purpose. Yes, sometimes it is extremely difficult to understand and acknowledge it, but God has planned how everything will work together to achieve His purpose for us. Experiencing and enduring the pain works as a catalyst that pushes you toward God. The pain is often excruciating, but God has promised that it all works together for good. Romans 8:28.

It is important to know that when we have reached "point give-up" that God steps in and carries us the rest of the way. It is God's intention to propel us perpetually to the next level of knowing who He truly is. That is the ultimate purpose behind the pain.

Even though pain has a way of knocking you down to your knees, trusting God has the power to lift you to a place in Him that will enable you to see brighter days. *"Your latter shall be greater than your past."* Haggai 2:9. In this life, there will always be pain -- but it's a small price to pay for the huge sacrifice that Jesus Christ made for us. Everything that happens in your life happens for a greater purpose.

I have come a long way from a near-death experience to be the woman of God that He has ordained. *"Before I formed you in the womb, I knew you. Before you were born, I set you apart, I appointed you as a prophet to the nations."* Jeremiah 1:5.

"I love the Lord for He heard my voice; the Lord heard my cry for mercy. Because He turned His ear to me, I will call on the Lord as long as I live. The cords of death entangled me, the anguish of the grave came over me; I was overcome by trouble and sorrow. Then I called on the name of the Lord. Save me! The Lord is gracious and righteous; our God is full of compassion. The Lord protects the unwary; when I was brought low, He saved me." Psalm 116-1-6.

As you continue to read my story, you may ask yourself, "How can I find my purpose? How can the pain I feel achieve God's plan for my life? In the midst of everything I have gone through, how can God use me?"

Even in the midst of turbulent times, all things are possible with God. Believe and trust Him even when darkness surrounds you. He has an abundant life waiting for you!

I pray that you will evaluate your life and realize that you too have a purpose.

REV. DR. NELLIE TAYLOR-WALTHRUST

ACKNOWLEDGMENTS

My sincere thanks and all praises to God for not giving up on me and for allowing me time and time again to discover who He sees me to be; a woman of purpose. I am thankful that I didn't give up on myself because I surely would have missed out on all that God created me to be: a proud wife, mother, and mentor.

Many thanks to my husband Elliott and to our wonderful sons, Thomas and Immanuel, who have always been an encouragement and a blessing to me. Thanks to Dr. Roseline Felix and Darnell Kennedy for their prayers and inspiration over the years and for reaching out to me during challenging times. To all my family, friends, and extended church family, thank you for your words of wisdom and support.

A special thank you to my pastor, Rev. Stephen Samuel, for unselfishly teaching and preaching the Word of God. You have made an impact on my life that can never be erased.

Thank you to Bishop Roderick R. Caesar and Pastor Beverly Caesar-Sherrod for seeing something in me that I didn't see in myself. I knew there was a special call from God on my life to preach the Gospel of Jesus Christ. Thank you for mentoring me. I appreciate your prayers and words of advice to ensure that I kept moving forward in the ministry to fulfill God's purpose. I have been blessed beyond measure to witness all that God has done in the lives of His people.

Thank you to Pastor Beverly Caesar for being the inspiration for me to tell my story. To the team and staff of *ZizaCreative Publishing* for your professional editing and artistic skills, thank you for your valuable input.

And thanks to all of you who will be reading *I Am My Mother's Daughter: The Purpose, The Pain, and The Shame.* I pray that a word of encouragement will leap from these pages and catapult you into fulfilling your God-given purpose.

Rev. Dr. Nellie Taylor-Walthrust
Long Island, New York | April, 2015

INTRODUCTION

I Am My Mother's Daughter: The Purpose, The Pain, and The Shame is an inside look into the author's early years. She speaks of her traumatic childhood experiences to relay a message of hope and inspiration. Throughout her account, she reassures the reader that everyone has a purpose in life. She makes it clear that God can use life's challenges to make you stronger and to fulfill His purpose. She advises readers to take comfort in God and to trust that He is working in their lives in times of tribulation. She also encourages them to use their personal experiences to minister to others.

The book begins with some insight into her mother's life story; her tremendous pain and struggle, particularly with postpartum depression. The effects of this disorder were so hard on her judgment that she comes close to killing her baby girl. The author relates how her mother surmounted difficult times through the support of her family and by her own determination starts her life over after making some bad choices. Through the analysis of her mother's story, she realizes the anguish that a young mother can go through when dealing with a relationship breakup, strong religious family values and other life circumstances while raising young children. What she communicates through her mother's story is *not to give up* when facing challenges. In spite of painful circumstances, she believes that hope, faith and trust in God can help you to prevail and move forward.

Chapters 4 through 7 speak of her mother's illness and passing, and the impact of growing up without her. She expounds on some of her hurdles while growing up, including an identity crisis as well as the need for approval and acceptance that she never received from her grandmother. In these chapters, however, she focuses on the possibility of prevailing over difficult experiences with proper adult intervention, guidance and nurturing.

In the last five chapters, the author speaks of her struggles involving being teased at school and how she escaped through her love for reading. She later relates her painful experience in a marriage of domestic violence.

She talks about the importance of positive people who were part of her life and the support she gained as a result of interacting with them. Being aware of your talents and gifts is a message that she imparts in the book. She concludes by offering *Seven Points of Healing* for the reader to apply and to gain a greater sense of self-worth.

The book provides valuable information on the impact and effects of a catastrophic childhood event. Nellie's life story delivers a powerful message of God's love. She emphasizes the importance of trusting God in the midst of heartache and reveals the importance of caring adult intervention in a child's life. Using her personal experiences - she demonstrates that in spite of the drawbacks and difficulties you may go through - life can become better again. As she tells her life story, she uses passages from the Bible as points of reference to show the source of her strength and courage.

Though the book touches only briefly on domestic violence and its effects on a relationship, it captures your attention with its straightforward, compelling narrative. The information that the author provides in this heartfelt and honest story can be valuable to young mothers facing similar life challenges. Healthcare professionals may find it useful as a starting point for discussion with children and young adults. Social workers, pastors, and counselors may also find it an effective resource to share.

Reverend Dr. Nellie Taylor-Walthrust has received a Doctorate in Ministry in Christian Theology and a Master's Degree in Christian Counseling. She is an ordained minister who has served for 20 years at Westbury Gospel Tabernacle in Long Island, New York. She is also the Director of the Leeds Place North Shore Child and Family Guidance Center where she has worked for 25 years. Nellie has a generous heart. She loves helping people improve their lives by discovering their true purpose and potential.

Dr. Roseline Felix
Colleague and Friend

I AM MY MOTHER'S DAUGHTER

MY BELOVED MOTHER

Olivia Taylor was born January 12, 1918 to the parentage of John Henry Taylor and Bessie Morton Taylor. She was affectionately called, *"Libby"* by her parents and everyone else who knew her. Olivia was the younger of two children. Irvin Taylor, her brother, was born January 9, 1917. Irvin was born blind as well as intellectually disabled. Early in life, Libby emerged as the protector, playmate and caregiver for her disabled brother. A special bond developed between them that lasted until Irvin's death at age thirty-five.

When Libby was ten years old, her mother Bessie passed away, leaving her two young children Olivia and Irvin. Her father, John, met and married Martha Hayes-Taylor, who quickly stepped into the role as mother to Bessie's two children. From the union of John Henry Taylor and Martha Hayes-Taylor, six children were born: Dorothy, James, Hampton, Roy, Lonnie, and Leila.

Being the oldest daughter, Olivia had a great love and compassion for her siblings; all of them looked up to her. She was always there to guide, encourage, inspire, protect and care for their physical and emotional needs. Libby was described as the *great protector*. Her siblings could count on her to be in their corner in the time of need.

Olivia attended a one-room schoolhouse located in the Gela Community about a 3-mile walk from Lewis Community where she lived. Education was not a priority among most African American families during the early 1900's. Olivia had seventh to eighth grade education, which was about the maximum standard for her era.

Olivia and her siblings who were of school age attended school only a few months each year. The girls attended school more regularly than the boys. The boys or young men of the family were required to stay home to work the farm during planting and harvesting seasons.

Olivia's father was one of the few farmers who owned his land. The Taylor family owned 59 acres of land, which was purchased by her grandfather on November 16, 1891 at the cost of $595.00. The land was designated as *heir property* and was passed down from generation to generation. This designation remains in effect even to this day.

Family members who grew up with Olivia described her as a quiet, easy-going, soft-spoken person. Even though she did not talk a lot, she was very articulate. When she did have a conversation with anyone, her approach was always humble, compassionate and loving, never harsh or rude. Everyone delighted to be in her presence. Olivia was described as the family peacemaker and confidant.

At the age of 20, Olivia was ready to start a life of her own. She left the safety of her parents and siblings and moved to the city of Durham, North Carolina, which was about 30 miles from her hometown of Oxford, North Carolina. Olivia's first cousin Flossie, who was also her best friend, came along with her. There they were: two young women living on their own - working, making their own money and enjoying the single life.

Olivia and Flossie obtained employment at Duke University Hospital, as it is known today. Duke Hospital, as it was known then, was the largest and most modern medical facility in the State of North Carolina. It was also one of the few employers that employed African Americans as para-professionals. Olivia was trained at Duke Hospital as a Nursing Assistant and provided patient care alongside registered nurses at the hospital. Being a Nursing Assistant was Olivia's only professional work history. Her employment at Duke Hospital extended over a three-year period.

Olivia's life quickly changed when she met and married her first husband, William Marrow. To this union, three sons were born: William, Melvin and Harold; and one daughter, Dorothy, who passed away at the age of eighteen months.

Prior to the devastating loss of her baby daughter, Olivia appeared to have had a very good and solid relationship with her husband. She seemed to enjoy making a healthy and happy life for herself and her family. William was described as a loving husband who adored his wife; he was a loving father to their three sons, as well as a great provider for his family. Family life was important to both of them.

Motherhood was something Olivia cherished. She and her stepmother, Martha, were pregnant at the same time. Olivia was pregnant with her first child, and her stepmother was pregnant with her last child. Olivia gave birth to her first son on January 1, 1940 and her stepmother gave birth to her last child, a daughter on July 22, 1940.

Olivia was happy to have the support of her family and her husband as she embraced motherhood. She transitioned quickly and easily into being a full-time mother and homemaker. She gave birth to three sons, each being about two years apart in age. To complete her family, she desired to have a daughter to balance their three sons. The birth of her baby daughter, Dorothy, was such a delight to her and her husband, just as her three sons were to the family. She wanted to honor her oldest sister by naming her baby daughter after her, whose name was Dorothy. They felt happy and complete as a family, but something wasn't quite right. The baby of their dreams had health issues that were never disclosed by anyone in the family.

This was a devastating loss and was not revealed to me until well into my adult life. My middle brother Harold shared with me that our mother had given birth to four children, and the fourth child was a baby girl who passed away at the age of eighteen months. He remembered her as their little sister but never knew the cause of her death.

The death of her baby daughter had a tremendous mental and emotional impact on Olivia as a young mother. This is believed to have started the decline in her relationship with her husband. Little was known about maternal depression, postpartum depression, major depression and its effects on a mother after the birth, and then the death of a child. By today's standards and available information on mood disorders, Olivia suffered in silence from a treatable emotional illness - severe postpartum depression.

However, other family members alleged that there were also infidelity issues in the marriage that led to the actual breakup. That was the family secret Olivia never shared, even though she knew firsthand that her husband was unfaithful in the bond of marriage.

Saddened by the loss of her baby daughter as well as the divorce from her husband, Olivia left the family home, leaving behind her three sons in the care of their father.

Olivia returned to the home of her parents a broken and depressed woman.

It appeared that her sadness had been compounded by loss after loss. Her past began with the death of her mother at an early age and the loss of her baby daughter. She and her husband divorced and even though they remained in the care of their father it seemed that Olivia had also lost her three sons.

But in spite of all that she suffered, my mother was a strong woman. Having been divorced, remarried and raising three children, she was still trying to maintain a relationship with her three older sons. It wasn't easy being an African American woman living in the South (North Carolina) during the early 1950's. It took a special woman to endure the social, mental and emotional challenges that she was faced with each day.

With her upbringing in a Christian home, divorce was frowned upon, and having two children out of wedlock spoiled the family values and moral standards that she had been taught as a child. Yet, in spite of what the social norms and family expectations might have been, Olivia stood tall and maintained her dignity and integrity as a woman of essence. Her gentle, kind, loving and sweet demeanor was always a welcome gift to her family and friends.

As I learned about how she dealt with all of these experiences, I gained a wealth of knowledge about her personality. My uncles, Hampton and James, and her best friend and closest confidant, cousin Flossie, all spoke of her humility, compassion and love for others. Olivia was often described as a person with so much love in her heart. Her smile and quiet demeanor would light the hearts of everyone who came in contact with her.

Even though her family didn't agree with many of her decisions and choices, they were always there to support her with unconditional love, caring and encouragement.

They were great examples of what the Bible teaches in Matthew 7:1-2, *"Do not judge or you too will be judged. For in the same way you judge others, you will be judged, and the same measure you use, it will be measured to you."* And in I Peter 4:8, *"Above all, love each other deeply, because love covers a multitude of sins."*

Perhaps the best compliment I have ever received from family members and friends that knew my mother is to say that *not only do I look like my mother, but I have the same character traits, the same smile and even sound like her when I speak.* Yes, I am my mother's daughter.

STARTING OVER

After experiencing challenges and tragedies, starting over can be extremely difficult. However, it is possible even when we are not making all the right choices. Olivia struggled with feelings that all was lost; feelings of being a failure. She asked herself, "What did I do wrong? When and where do I start to rebuild my life? Is it wrong or bad to start over? Who will understand and support me in my efforts?"

When faced with feelings of having been so close to achieving your life's goals and dreams and then losing so much, starting over can seem overwhelming. Those emotions can lead to temptations that I am quite sure she thought she had conquered early in life. But then, later in life, the root of the same tests and trials had surfaced. Realizing that she was beginning from ground zero spurred that motherly instinct to love and nurture and to have the same affections returned to her.

In just a short span of time after her divorce, those emotions led to "looking for love in all the wrong places." A brief affair with a young man led to a pregnancy and soon to the birth of a baby girl, Minnie. Fourteen months later, after another affair with a different young man, Olivia again gave birth to a baby girl, Nellie. There she was, a beautiful young woman – a single parent with two baby girls born out of wedlock – living at home with her father and stepmother. Life was not looking too prosperous for her.

Her choices had dishonored her family and all the moral values she had been taught during her upbringing. Compounded by her emotional state of maternal and postpartum depression after the birth of her second daughter Nellie, she became so distraught that she threatened to kill her baby girl. But, through divine intervention, her baby girl was saved from being brutally killed by her stepmother.

I grew up hearing this story all of my young life. My grandmother would often tell me that I wasn't a *wanted* child; that *nobody wanted me*, not even my mother. She would say this especially when she was angry or upset about any attention-seeking behavior that I may have been exhibiting. For years my thought was, "Yes, I was that little girl who my mother almost killed."

My grandmother's story:

> *One day when you were only a few days old, your mother took you outside in a cornfield that was near the back door of our country farmhouse. She placed you on the ground; then she picked up a large rock. Just as she was about to smash your head with that rock, I called out to her and said, "Libby don't you hurt that baby, bring her to me." Libby complied, put down the rock, picked you up and handed you over to me.*

She concluded the story with:

> *"...and don't you ever forget; if it had not been for me, you would be dead, and the buzzards would have picked your bones."*

Oh! How I wish the story ended there, and we all lived happily ever after. But as you continue to read my story, you will see how this event impacted my life as a child and into adulthood.

The circumstances following my birth presented many years of shame, embarrassment and confusion. It was my understanding and belief, especially being the mother of two sons - that a new baby is supposed to bring joy and happiness to a mother's heart. That had been my experience after the birth of my sons.

The story of my birth was the complete opposite. As I tried to make sense of being an unwanted baby at birth, there seemed to be no logical explanation. I came to the conclusion and accepted wholeheartedly that there was something wrong with me so troubling to my mother that she felt she could not cope with during that time in her life. Difficult family and personal issues had caused her great emotional pain. The thought never entered my mind that my mother could have been suffering from a mental health disorder.

Thirty-five years into my career as a mental health professional, I heard about a disorder that affects women of childbearing age before and after childbirth. The disorder is called *maternal depression and postpartum depression*. My eagerness to learn more about it led me to do extensive reading and research to educate and increase my personal knowledge about the cause and effects of this disorder.

The more I read, the more the missing pieces of the puzzle began to fit together. Practically every article revealed a symptom or behavior that my mother had exhibited prior to and after my birth. As an adult, I was now making sense of the behavior and impaired judgment that I had only heard about years before.

With my newfound information, I was suddenly stricken with mixed emotions. Firstly, I experienced a sense of relief that there wasn't something so bad about me after all. Secondly, I was sad and grieved that my mother never knew why she felt and acted the way she did to her newborn baby. Thirdly, my grandmother did not know or have any level of understanding of what my mother was experiencing in the aftermath of childbirth.

I don't know what my mother's faith was during this difficult time, but I do believe that Jesus prayed for us. I do believe that God used my grandmother to stop the plan of the enemy for both our lives. The outcome could have been that my mother would be institutionalized in a mental hospital or a correctional facility for murder. And I would have been dead, never to enjoy the gracious life that God has given me.

"The cords of death entangled me; the anguish of the grave came upon me; I was overcome by trouble and sorrow. (v.8) The Lord delivered me from death... (v.9) I will walk before the Lord in the land of the living." Psalm 116:3, 8-9.

three

READY TO MOVE FORWARD

Olivia was being tested in so many ways. In all of the trials she experienced, some tests she passed and others she failed. In spite of it all, God's mercy, forgiveness and faithfulness gave her another chance at true love. I believe the one lesson she learned was not to give up when you fail to handle a challenge or can't find the solution to a problem. Giving up can only develop into another problem. When you are facing difficult issues, it is a clear indication that God is speaking to you. With each circumstance, you can know that there is a message of hope, trust and faith.

The year 1952 was a turning point in Olivia's life. She married her second husband, Reuben Daniels. He was a gentle, kind and loving man who absolutely adored her and was equally as accepting and loving toward her two daughters, Minnie and Nellie. He was hard working; a great provider who only wanted to make his new wife and family happy. As a token of his love for Olivia, he gave her a half-karat diamond engagement ring and a gold Bulova watch, which she wore proudly. Gifts like this were a real sacrifice for a sharecropper's income.

Reuben was welcomed favorably by Olivia's family. Olivia was equally welcomed into her new husband's family. Everyone wanted to see her happiness restored. She was readily accepted and shown love and respect, even though she was bringing a lot of past history into the marriage. She was a divorced mother of three sons and the mother of two young daughters born out of wedlock.

Reuben had only unconditional love for his wife and never judged her for her past. Reuben had no previous marriage or children. Olivia was the center of his joy, which he openly shared with everyone who knew them as a couple.

My greatest memory of my mother, even though I was only two and a half years old, was our first Christmas together as a family. My stepfather, working as a sharecropper, moved our family into a small house that was owned by the farmer for whom he worked. In my photographic memory, I remember the house being a log-cabin like structure with only two rooms, a large bedroom and a kitchen. The bedroom was the main living space in the house. It had a wood- burning fireplace that was used to heat the entire house.

It was Christmas Eve and I remember the large fireplace glowing with a bright red fire. Across the room, stood a tall Christmas tree that my mother had decorated with a variety of colorful Christmas ornaments. While my sister and I slept in our bed together, Santa Claus made his visit.

On Christmas morning, I awoke to see many gifts around the Christmas tree. My sister and I received identical blue and white tricycles that only differed in size to fit a three-and-a-half year old and a two-and-a-half year old. A red metal telephone sat on the seat of each tricycle and a beautiful baby doll rested against our tricycles along with a shoebox of Christmas confectioneries of candy, assorted nuts, apples, oranges and raisins. What a great Christmas it was! It was everything that two little girls could ever dream of.

Olivia was six months pregnant and on March 24, 1953 she gave birth to a baby boy, Reuben, Jr. This was one of the happiest times in her new life. Starting over and moving forward after experiencing hard circumstances was part of the journey, which led to her becoming more mature. It allowed her to take another step forward knowing that she was prepared to live out the purpose of God for her life. She had built a new family, the exact number of children from her first marriage. She had a loving husband, two daughters and a newborn son.

When I think of the short life span of my mother, I find comfort in this Scripture:

> *"Consider it pure joy, my brothers, whenever you face trials of many kinds, because you know that the testing of your faith develops perseverance. Perseverance must finish its work so that you may be mature and complete, not lacking anything." James 1:2-4.*

I AM MY MOTHER'S DAUGHTER

four
THE FINAL TRANSITION

Olivia became ill shortly after the birth of my baby brother Reuben, Jr. She was diagnosed with Malignant Hypertension, which is extremely high blood pressure that develops rapidly and causes severe organ damage. Malignant Hypertension affected my mother's kidneys thereby causing kidney failure. This condition required her to make frequent visits to Duke Hospital located in Durham, North Carolina. This was the same hospital where she had worked as a Nursing Assistant in the beginning of her young adult life.

After several months of treatment without any favorable prognosis, my mother accepted the reality that her life expectancy was going to be short. As a young child, I remember my grandmother had often told me about her final preparation to go to the hospital for another treatment. She knew it was going to be my mother's final visit.

In her last conversation with my grandmother, my mother said that she would not be coming back home. In her words, she requested, "take care of my three little children." She then removed her diamond ring from her finger and gave it to my grandmother with instructions to give it to my sister Minnie when she became of age. Then she removed her gold watch from her wrist and instructed my grandmother to give her watch to Nellie when she became of age. Finally, she told my grandmother where to find her pink gold earrings, two pairs that were located in the bottom of her cedar chest. Her instructions were to give each one of her girls a pair of earrings when they were old enough to wear them. She wanted each of us to remember her in a special way.

Olivia said goodbye to her three little children and then got into the back seat of the car that was taking her to the hospital. As the car drove off, she continued to look out of the back window and wave goodbye to my grandmother and her three little children. Everyone watched until the car was completely out of view.

On October 18, 1953, Olivia departed this life peacefully at the age of 35 with her loving husband Reuben at her bedside. Left to cherish her memory were her six children from age 12 years to six months. Grieving her passing was her loving husband, her father, stepmother, and seven siblings including her developmentally challenged brother Irvin whom she loved so dearly.

The death of Olivia at such a young age was a tremendous and unexpected loss to her family and friends. Her family had been prayerful and was expecting Olivia to be cured of the illness and return home to enjoy her new life.

I believe God had a greater plan because earth wasn't the place for her. God needed an angel in heaven and He chose an earthly angel named Olivia.

"We also rejoice in our sufferings, because we know that suffering produces perseverance; perseverance, character; and character, hope and hope does not disappoint us." Romans 5:3-5.

THE FUNERAL

How do you prepare six little children to say a final goodbye to their mother? As my stepfather prepared for the funeral, it was his desire that all of my mother's children attend, especially her three sons who were in the care of their father and her first husband.

A question that remains unanswered to this present day is: *"Why was my third oldest brother, Harold - age eight at the time - not allowed to attend the funeral?"* Years later, as we shared our childhood stories together, he always wondered why his father William told him to stay home on the morning of the funeral while his two older brothers were taken to the funeral.

Families deal with death and dying in different ways. Often the emotional separation clouds your better judgment, leaving unanswered questions and hurt feelings. Maybe this was the reason for William's decision - I don't know.

I was only three years old, but my mind still pictures the day of the funeral as if it happened yesterday. My mother's favorite color was pink. She was buried in an all pink gown and a white casket lined with pink satin. I remember sitting on the front seat of the church (Stovall Baptist Church) between my stepfather and my grandmother. When it was time for the final viewing, the funeral director picked me up so that I could see my mother for the last time.

It was a late fall day, and it was typical in the South for the weather to get very chilly in the late afternoon. My sister and I were taken from the church and placed in the front seat of the hearse that would take my mother's remains to the cemetery. This was very frightening to me because I had never seen someone dressed in all black. Most of all, I didn't have my mother there to calm my fears, with her loving arms to hug me and lift me to her lap, and to reassure me that everything was alright. Perhaps this was my first experience with separation anxiety and the feeling of abandonment.

Just before my mother's remains were lowered into the ground, with the casket about halfway down, the funeral director came to the hearse to take my sister and me to the gravesite. Once again, I was picked up by this man dressed in black. I was told to look down into the grave to get a final view of my mother's casket. As the sun set over her grave on that late fall day in October so did my memory of that day end.

Later in life I came to understand that my mother had fulfilled the purpose God had for her life. As short as her life was, she left a legacy and many precious memories that will be shared for generations to come. I'm so glad to be a part of her story and proud to be my mother's daughter.

six

WOULD LIFE BE "NORMAL" AGAIN?

After the promise my grandmother had made to my mother to take care of her three little children, I couldn't understand what was happening next. Within a few weeks, we became foster children; six of us living in different homes. My older brothers remained in the care of their father. My six-month old brother, my sister, and I were placed in the home of my grandfather's brother Sterling and his wife, Elizabeth. It is still unclear how this arrangement came about.

However, in the early 1950's, it was extremely difficult for anyone to care for three small children financially and to take care of their own family. Even though my grandfather and grandmother were the most financially able to care for us, a decision was made to let us go into the care of Uncle Buster and Aunt Sis, as they were affectionately called. We remained in their care for approximately six months. Then suddenly one day, Uncle Buster and Aunt Sis told my sister and me that we were going back to live with my maternal grandparents in the rural community of Lewis, five miles from the city limits of Oxford, North Carolina. Meanwhile, my baby brother remained in their care until he was about 18 months old.

My stepfather took guardianship of little Reuben, and they moved to Stovall, North Carolina, about five miles from where we lived in the Lewis Community. My stepfather along with his two sisters, Arlene and Isabelle took the best care of my little brother. Even though we lived in three separate households, we always knew about each other. My stepfather remained an integral part of my life until his death in 1969.

Life on the farm with my grandparents was a lot different from life with Uncle Buster and Aunt Sis. Immediately we were given chores like gathering firewood to put in the wood-burning stove to cook the meals and heat the house in the winter. We had to attend to the farm animals, work in the tobacco fields, harvest fruits and vegetables and help with the laundry for the family. There were many chores for us to do at such a young age.

By the time my sister and I arrived at my grandparents' house, all of my mother's siblings had left the family home except her youngest sister Lelia. They were young adults living on their own. Some had moved to New York and some to Pennsylvania to have a better quality of life. Farming and sharecropping were the only jobs available for African Americans at that time. Segregation was the glass ceiling. People of color had no rights in the South during that era.

By the time I reached age five, I knew that there was a big void in my life. Even though my basic needs were being met, my social and emotional needs were not. It was obvious that there was a clear and distinct difference between the way I was treated as a child and the way my sister was treated. My sister was highly favored by my grandmother. Meanwhile my grandfather, a very stern and no-nonsense man, was equally caring and nurturing to both of us.

My self-esteem and my self-image were non-existent. I was extremely shy, very clingy; always seeking to be accepted and shown the same love and affection that my grandmother so openly and generously lavished upon my sister.

Whenever I exhibited any childlike, attention-seeking behavior, my grandmother would harshly reprimand me with the story of my birth. While scolding me verbally, she would say, "Nobody wanted you, not even your mother. If it had not been for me, you would be dead, and the buzzards would have picked your bones." These words drove me further into isolation. Nobody wanted me as a baby and still four years later, nobody wanted me. With hurt feelings, I learned to self-soothe by playing alone under our house and talking to imaginary friends. I spent many hours and long days daydreaming about what life would have been like if my mother was alive. Would she not want me now? Would she tell me she loved me? Perhaps she really didn't love me. Maybe I would have been better off if she had carried out her plan to kill me.

I spent many days and sleepless nights trying to understand what my grandmother meant when she always concluded her scolding with, "...and the buzzards would pick your bones." I knew what a buzzard was because I would always see these large black birds flying overhead looking for any kind of dead animal whose flesh they could devour and leave only the bones or carcass. My only explanation for my grandmother's harsh statement was that if I was dead or if I died I wasn't worthy of a burial like other people. She would be satisfied just leaving me to be another meal for these birds of prey.

My grandmother refused to pamper me in any way. She always insisted that I could take care of whatever needs I may have had. This forced me more into isolation and to figure out how I was going to take care of myself as an unwanted child. I had to grow up sooner than I wanted to. I wanted her undivided attention and her approval. I wanted her acceptance and for her to show me unconditional love. I wanted to belong and to feel that she loved me as much as she did my sister.

Whenever she made reference to the color of my skin or the texture of my hair it affirmed what I had been told – nobody wanted me because these were things that I didn't know how to change. It was as though everyone was expecting a different looking girl, and I just happened to have been *the accident* that nobody was ready for. I was not a carbon copy of my sister who was fair-skinned and had a "better" texture of hair than I had. My sister was extremely vocal and outgoing yet I was extremely shy and non-verbal. It was as though I didn't exist at all.

By the time I reached age four, I was practically non-verbal. I didn't have to speak; whenever I was greeted or spoken to by family or friends, my grandmother would always answer with, "she doesn't talk." I am still not sure why she would not allow me to respond for myself even though she knew I could talk even with my soft voice and shy ways.

Perhaps she thought I wasn't intelligent enough to answer, or maybe she didn't want anyone to notice me. Maybe she was ashamed of me or angry because she had to keep a close watch on me. Perhaps it was because I was born with an undeveloped esophagus, which made it difficult for me to swallow solid food and liquids causing me to choke easily and unexpectedly.

There is one thing that I am sure of - in the southern family - you never undermine or disrespect what an adult said. If you spoke when they said you could not, you would be punished for being disrespectful. So, I learned not to speak and simply looked to my grandmother who always answered for me. I grew to love this arrangement because at least I thought she was protecting me from intrusive people. I only wanted to be the most perfect and obedient child in the whole world just to please my grandmother. It was later in life when I learned that this had a major negative impact on the development of my verbal, social and emotional skills.

In spite of the harsh verbal abuse that I was subjected to, I never stopped seeking love and affection from my grandmother. I just wanted her to accept me as a little girl who needed unconditional love. I never gave up hope because I truly loved her and I always wanted to be near her. I wanted to bond with a loving and caring adult. But, this was a void that she wasn't able to or willing to fill.

If there is a lesson to be learned in the midst of despair, it would be to learn to accept your uniqueness. Search within yourself to find the special gifts, talents and abilities that our Creator has given to each of us. Make an assessment of your strengths and with the help of God maximize what He has given you to the fullest extent. Never measure or compare yourself to others because there is only one you. Emphasize the things that you do well and learn to manage those things that are more challenging for you.

"Consider it pure joy, my brothers, whenever you face trials of many kinds because you know that the testing of your faith develops perseverance. Perseverance must finish its work so that you may be mature and complete, not lacking anything." James 1:2-4.

One of the key words used in this Scripture is *perseverance*. Perseverance is the act of enduring in spite of opposition or discouragement caused by your circumstances. Perseverance is the renewed mind to overcome the thoughts of failing and the guarded heart to work through the emotional pain. It is the shedding of tears when you cannot find the words to say as well as the strength you find in God when your weakness has become unbearable.

I AM MY MOTHER'S DAUGHTER

seven

MY CHILDHOOD YEARS

By the time I was six years old and ready to start first grade, I was like a *fish out of water*. I had no social or verbal skills. This was the first time in my life that I wasn't attached or dependent upon my grandmother to cover all of my verbal, social and emotional needs. School adjustment was very hard. I wanted to engage with my fellow peers; I wanted to make friends. I wanted to play with my classmates. I wanted to have conversations with my teachers, but I did not know how. I only knew how to isolate myself.

I recall during recess when all of my classmates were running and playing and having a wonderful time together. I could be found crying, standing alone near a tree. When approached and asked by my teacher what was wrong, I would say, "Nobody wants to play with me." Immediately, my teacher would call a group of girls over and tell them to include me in their play. They would take my hand and we would all walk away to join the other children who were busy playing jump rope, kickball, duck-duck goose, and hide-and-go-seek. Playtime and being with my classmates was like being in heaven. A completely new world was opened up to me. However, it was only good for that day. The cycle would repeat itself the very next day because I didn't know how to initiate or engage in play with others.

I am truly grateful for wonderful teachers who identified my issues immediately and worked fervently to address them by physically teaching me how to interact with my classmates and other students. The first drill that I remember being taught by my first grade teacher was: (1) identify the activity that interests you (2) walk over to the group (3) do not look down at the ground (4) ask, "May I play with you?" It always worked. I can't recall ever being rejected. Sometimes I was asked to wait until the game started again, but I was always included.

I was blessed with excellent academic skills. I loved school. It was my goal each year to have perfect attendance and make the honor roll, which I achieved almost every year from first grade to twelfth grade. In elementary school, I excelled in reading, math, spelling, and science. By the time I completed first grade, the tide was beginning to change. My grandparents began to acknowledge that I was a better student academically than my sister. I learned practically everything from her because she was only a grade ahead, and it was easier for her to share with me what she had learned the previous year. I was a quick learner and was able to retain information, which made me a very good test taker.

One of my favorite activities was making science projects. I was extremely knowledgeable about the outdoors. I could identify and name practically every creature and plant or tree found in nature.

Working alongside my grandfather, who was a highly esteemed farmer, I learned more about his character. He was someone most people feared because of his stern demeanor, but I quickly learned how gentle and loving he was. He was a great teacher. He had a way of making me feel as though I was the most special person in the world. He always praised me for the work I did and corrected me when it was not my best. This encouraged me to perfect every task that he assigned me to do. I wanted to be praised because that said to me that I was good at something; *you have value, you can be noticed and you have self-worth.* This validation said to me, *"Yes, I am good at something; therefore, I must be loved for what I'm doing."*

I enjoyed learning from my grandmother also. She was an excellent southern cook. She would use mostly fruits, vegetables and meats that were grown on our farm to make meals that were extremely delicious. My grandmother did not allow children in her kitchen while she was cooking. She did allow me to assist her in the preparation of the foods that she was going to prepare for a meal or preserve for future use. She saw my interest in learning how to cook so she would allow me to climb on a chair and watch while she did the cooking. I learned by watching, and by the age of ten, I was able to prepare complete meals for the family. I loved cooking and some of my skills exceeded my grandmother's.

> *"Train a child in the way he should go, and when he is old,*
> *he will not turn from it." Proverbs 22:6.*

I AM MY MOTHER'S DAUGHTER

eight
BUILDING SELF-ESTEEM

Friedrich Nietzsche (1844-1900), a German-Swiss philosopher and writer wrote: "At bottom, every man knows well enough that he is a unique being, only once on this earth, and by no extraordinary chance will such a marvelously picturesque piece of diversity in unity as he is, ever be put together a second time."

An unknown author once said: "Think highly of yourself, for the world takes you at your own estimate."

Marie Downey, whom I adopted as my godmother, came into my life when I was age eight or nine. She was the center of my life until age 14 when she and her family moved away from the Lewis Community to another part of the city of Oxford, North Carolina. She was a young mother of ten children, but ten wasn't enough. Her unconditional love extended to an eleventh child when I became "her baby," as she would always call or refer to me.

Marie was a full-time mother and housewife caring for her family, but she found time every day to visit my grandparents just to come and check on me. Her daily visit was the most exciting part of my day. My heart would almost leap out of my body when I saw her coming. When she arrived at our house, she would say hello and then ask, "Where is my baby?" referring to me. Oh! What joy it was to be held on her loving lap, hugged tightly, kissed on the cheek and told, "you are my baby and I love you." Not only was she special to me, but she was also special to my grandparents. She would always pitch in to help them with whatever they were doing. She would help my grandmother by doing work around the house, or if we were working in the tobacco field with my grandfather, she would join in and help us until the job was completed.

Marie was a true mother to me. She filled the voids that had been empty for many years. She took pride in combing my hair and putting beautiful ribbons on my braids. She would bring me clothing more appropriate for a little girl. After each visit, her parting words were, "Don't let anyone tell you that you are not beautiful because you are beautiful and very special to me." That made my heart glad because I truly believed in her and I trusted her to tell me the truth. She knew firsthand that my grandmother treated me differently because she favored my sister over me. Marie was my solid rock and my strong source of encouragement.

Marie became a widow at a very young age when her husband suddenly passed away, and she was left to raise ten children on her own. In spite of her challenges to be a mother and father to her ten children, she never forgot about me. Her love extended into adulthood as one of the most influential persons in my life. She gave unconditional love or what I call *agape* love, which is the kind of love that comes from the Lord Jesus Christ. Marie looked beyond my faults; whether they were real or just my emotional state of mind. She saw a little girl who was lonely, abandoned and deprived of a mother's love. She gave so much, even to the point that I don't think she realized the impact she had on my life. Even now, I believe she is still looking down from Heaven upon my life. I bless God for Marie; she will be treasured in my heart forever. I believe God put her in my life with a purpose to help me succeed in life and become the person He created me to be. I could not have reached my full potential without somebody else believing in me the way she did.

The Bible says that love is kind, which means that love looks for ways to help improve someone else's life. Marie was never more like God than when she gave unselfishly. The closest thing to the heart of God is helping others. In the eyes of God she was a people builder; her only desire was to bring out the best in others. I know she cared about me that way.

If God did this for me, He can do the same for you. Trust Him and watch for the angel He has placed in your life! Only God can help you shake off those feelings of guilt and worthlessness.

I AM MY MOTHER'S DAUGHTER

.

nine
LEARNING TO LIKE MYSELF

Jesus said, in Matthew 19:19, *"Love your neighbor as you love yourself."* The prerequisite to loving others is to love yourself. How could I do this? All of my life I had been told, *"Nobody wants you, you are too black, your hair is too nappy, you are unlovable, you were an unwanted child from birth."* I believed every single negative thing that I was told by my grandmother. She was my caregiver; the closest person to me, and the authority on raising children. I never heard such negative descriptions about any of her sons or daughters, and certainly not about my older sister.

I was totally confused at this point in my life. But like any pre-adolescent girl I wanted to be loved. I wanted to be accepted and have a place of belonging within the heart of my grandmother. It was not difficult to love my grandmother. As a child, I only wanted to be accepted and to receive the tender touch of her hand on my face and her strong arms wrapped around my little body. I needed the comfort of climbing into her lap, but it never came. The searching and seeking never stopped.

During my years in grade school, I used to feel very bad when the older students, mostly high school students, would tease me about my appearance.

They teased me about my shyness, my lack of verbal communication skills and my frequent tears from hurt feelings. Sometimes I would hear them say awful things about my lunch bag and the contents of my lunch, which were greasy egg biscuits. Then there was the sudden tugging on my pigtails and quick denial that they didn't do it. And worst of all, having to stand up in the aisle of the school bus when students refused to allow me to sit down because they were holding seats for their friends.

With tears welling up in my eyes and a lump rising in my throat, how I wished I could simply disappear. My mind raced back and forth about the story that had been etched in my mind from home. I was totally unprepared for the cruelty of others. Even though no one ever picked fights with me, they did make fun of me. The sad part of this story is that even though I wanted to go home and cry on my grandmother's lap and look for her to comfort me, I knew that she wasn't available to me. I suppressed my emotions and suffered in silence.

I learned to counteract some of those feelings of being excluded, isolated and cut off from the normal things that most children enjoy in their young lives. My escape became reading. I developed a great love for it at a very early age. It seemed to come naturally to me, even though there was not much reading material in our house. I became very good at salvaging old newspapers and magazines from the neighborhood trash piles. I would rummage through the trash and take home as much reading material as my little arms could carry.

My first Bible storybook was one that I salvaged out of the trash pile. I remember reading the story of Jonah being swallowed up by a big whale where he stayed for three days and was then spit up alive on a beach. Each Bible story that I read became more and more exciting; the stories of Noah, Moses, the three Hebrew boys, David and Daniel being thrown into the lion's den and how God saved them all. That book became my pride and joy, and I looked forward to reading a Bible story every night before going to bed.

It was as though I was experiencing some of the same or similar hardships that these Bible characters had experienced in their lives. Yet, they were victorious and did great things to help others. Their stories gave me a sense of hope inwardly, but I dared not share what was going on in my head and my heart. I believed that any outward expression of feeling lonely would be viewed as opposing and disrespectful. It had been instilled in me at the onset of my life that *"children are to be seen and not heard."* I just wanted acceptance, but I wasn't going to say or do anything that resembled being disobedient.

The Bible storybook, the old newspapers, and the magazines became my personal treasures. I read each one from front to back and re-read them again and again until I was able to salvage more reading materials.

My love for reading was more than a comfort to me; it also helped me to develop my reading skills. It got me some personal attention from my grandfather who could not read or write. My grandfather would often listen as I read aloud to him. He never learned to read, but he did learn to write his name in script. This was a great accomplishment for him, instead of just placing an "X" on the dotted line, which was accepted on any document that required a signature. Very few African Americans born in the 1800's had any formal education. I taught my grandfather to write his name, *John Henry Taylor,* by holding his hand and tracing each letter until he learned how to form each letter of his name on his own. It was a proud moment for both of us.

I thank God for good elementary school teachers who helped me believe that I had an abundance of good qualities to every negative quality. Each teacher began to speak positive and encouraging words about my abilities: *you are determined, always on time, always willing to help others, you are courteous, kind, and respectful to others.* They assured me that I had great potential if I worked on being more assertive in communicating my wants and wishes to others.

They always reminded me that I was better than the students and the other people who constantly teased and made fun of me. They helped me to understand that sometimes people's reactions are a result of jealousy. Even when I wanted to retreat and was ready to give up, my teachers encouraged me to believe in myself and never give up. They encouraged me to "stick with it" because God made me in His likeness with unique gifts, talents, and abilities. The key to learning to love yourself is to manage your weaknesses and work hard on developing your strengths.

In I Corinthians 13:13, the Apostle Paul writes, *"Now these three remain: faith, hope, and love, but the greatest of these is love."*

In middle school, my eighth grade teacher, Mrs. Lucinda Poole began to mentor me. She saw that I needed help developing my emotional and social skills. Mrs. Poole was a gentle yet firm woman. She was a large full-figured woman who spoke with a very stern voice that immediately evoked fear in you. But there was a completely different side of her; she was warm, caring, nurturing, compassionate, giving and a great motivator.

Mrs. Poole was a widow and had no children of her own. However, she had great motherly love for children with physical and emotional needs. She voluntarily became the caregiver of a young girl whose parents could not financially provide for all their children. She was the best mother to her adopted daughter. There was such a motherly bond between them that I greatly admired and longed to have in my life.

Mrs. Poole was my trusted mentor. Not only did I have the highest regard for her, but my grandparents shared the same. She was the only person they trusted enough to allow me to stay with overnight. It was such a delight to spend weekends with her and her adopted daughter. I felt safe and emotionally connected to both of them. She allowed me to be myself, and I always felt special and welcomed by her and her family. Mrs. Poole was a strong emotional support to me.

She would have long conversations with me about my shy and withdrawn behavior. It was as though she was a therapist who knew every human behavior and how a person could bring about change simply by changing the way they think about themselves and their circumstances. She used phrases like: *"You can do it if you put your mind to it; never give up no matter what; you have a lot of God-given talent. Don't let your past block your success in the future."* What wisdom she had freely imparted to me! Much of what she told me, I didn't understand at the time, but it certainly sounded good and I treasured it in my heart.

In the most humble way, Mrs. Poole spoke to me about my school apparel. She knew that she could be a blessing without drawing any attention or making any negative reflection on my grandmother. She could clearly see that there was a big difference in my appearance compared to my sister. My school attire consisted of clothing worn in previous years by my sister; most of it wasn't in the greatest condition, but it was always clean and pressed.

In a quiet and dignified way, Mrs. Poole would call me aside at lunchtime and say, "I have a bag for you to take home today. Let your grandparents know that it's from me." After extending my sincere appreciation, I could hardly wait to get home to see my new clothing. Even though they were from her adopted daughter, they were very pretty and stylish, and I couldn't wait to wear them. I felt like a princess wearing a ball gown and golden slippers.

Because of Mrs. Poole's generosity, my middle school days were much more pleasant. I didn't stand out or draw negative attention to myself because of what I was wearing but instead admired by my classmates for my stylish attire.

My first big school social event happened while I was still a student in Mrs. Poole's eighth-grade class. Each year, my school would hold a big fundraising fall festival to raise money to purchase an activity bus for our school. Having an activity bus opened up new opportunities for students of color to participate in field trips, team sports like basketball and baseball, and music competitions.

The highlight of the festival was the crowning of *Ms. Harvest Festival Queen*. The student who donated the largest amount of tobacco bundles would be the winner. The tobacco that the students donated would be sold at the tobacco market, and the money would go towards the purchase of the activity bus. I was surprised to be the largest contributor of tobacco that year and was the winner! This was the first time that middle school students had ever won the title. It was always assumed that a high school student would be the winner. This caused some concern with the school's Harvest Festival Committee. So, it was decided that the high school student who was the second place runner-up would be crowned *queen*, and I would be given the role of first runner-up as an attendant in the *Queen's Court*. This was the first time I had ever been involved in such a prestigious event. I was just happy to be involved in a small way.

Mrs. Poole, my mentor and eighth-grade teacher, was so proud of me. She took the time to teach me everything I needed to know to be a poised eighth-grade representative.

On the evening of the event, I was accompanied to the festival by my sister and grandparents. They sat proudly in the audience awaiting my entrance, wearing the pretty blue party dress given to me by my favorite Auntie, Lelia. Perhaps this was the first time in my life when I was the center of attention and was acknowledged by my grandmother. I believe she looked at me that evening with a different perspective. Perhaps she realized there was something in me that deserved to be nurtured and developed.

It was through the encouragement of my teachers that I learned not to let others put limitations on me. But if you don't have a support system from parents or guardians, it can be difficult to overcome the negative labels that have been placed on you. The lesson I learned is that a person's perception of you is often *only* perception and not reality.

To make your dreams a reality, identify the strengths God has given you and use them:

- Let others know how you want to be treated and never compromise or settle for less.

- Explore and define your dreams and goals for your life.

- Seek out people who believe in you and support your dreams.

- Do not embrace negative people who try to limit you or discourage you from achieving your goals.

> *"I can do all things through Christ, which strengthens me."*
> *Philippians 4:13.*

I AM MY MOTHER'S DAUGHTER

MY SPIRITUAL ROOTS

Lewis Chapel United Church of Christ

The family that prays together stays together.

"Trust in the Lord with all your heart and lean not to your own understanding; in all your ways acknowledge Him and He will make your paths straight." Proverbs 3:5-6.

Unlike most households today, not going to church as a family wasn't an option for me as a child. Sunday worship was paramount in our house. Preparation for church began on Saturday afternoon. First, we heated large pots of water that were used to take a good soaking bath from head to toe. Next, your Sunday attire was appropriately selected and carefully checked to make sure it was clean and well pressed.

I looked forward to getting up early on Sunday morning to a country breakfast of smoked sausage, fried potatoes, scrambled eggs and buttermilk biscuits with fresh butter and homemade preserves. It wasn't uncommon to have smothered chicken with rich brown gravy served with biscuits and fried potatoes. Sunday morning breakfast was a real treat in the traditional southern family.

After a hearty breakfast, it was time to get dressed for Sunday school. My grandmother would dress my sister and me first and then have us sit on the front porch until she got dressed. Since we did not have a car, we had to walk quite a distance to get to our church. My grandmother, my sister and I would wear old shoes to walk the distance. When we approached the edge of the church grounds, we would change our old shoes and hide them under a bush as we slipped into our Sunday dress shoes. When the service was over we would again retrieve our old shoes for the walk back home.

Sunday school was exciting, and we attended every Sunday. There were many activities that I enjoyed like reading the Scriptures and memorizing Bible verses. Each Sunday, we had to recite a different Bible verse. My love for the Bible and especially Bible stories was ignited in Sunday School. Even though I was very shy and withdrawn, I loved taking in the information. Because of my shyness I reluctantly participated verbally because I was accustomed to not talking, and my grandmother had already informed everyone that I didn't talk. My Sunday school teacher knew otherwise because I always recited my Scripture verse perfectly each week. I practiced my Bible verse alone all week, talking to myself or to my imaginary friends. I always spoke in a very low, soft voice, but it was loud enough to be heard by my Sunday school teacher. She always praised me for a good job, which I loved to hear.

Most churches in the South did not have full worship services every Sunday. Worship service was held once a month at our church on the fourth Sunday. It was on this Sunday that all the members and community persons attended worship service. The fourth Sunday was a big deal. You wore your "Sunday Best" because this was the time that everyone was watching you as an individual and as a family. The family had to look as near perfect as possible.

Somehow, the fourth Sunday always seemed to be a problem for me. The excitement of the day was too much for me. In my excitement to be all dressed up in my "Sunday Best" and hearing the serious instructions from my grandmother to sit on the front porch while she got dressed, I somehow would get too close to the edge of the porch, trip over my feet and fall into the dirt. This behavior always brought a big scolding from my grandmother who had to clean me up and dust off my hair and clothing as best she could so that I would be presentable to go to church.

My grandfather, who was a serving deacon, always joined us at church on the fourth Sunday. On the other three Sundays of the month, he would visit different churches in the community while we attended Sunday school. It was mostly on the first Sunday of the month that my grandmother, my sister and I would join him for worship at the neighboring church (Hardy Grove Baptist Church).

My grandfather always arrived for church service elegantly dressed in his suit, starched white shirt, matching necktie and well-shined shoes. My grandfather would saddle his mule and ride it to church. When he reached the grounds of the church, he would dismount and tie the mule to a tree branch where it patiently waited until my grandfather returned for the ride back home.

Everyone in the family was actively involved in the various ministries of the church. My grandfather was a deacon and certainly a man of prayer. I always felt proud of him whenever he was asked to pray during the service. He prayed from his heart. I know now that it was the Holy Spirit who gave him utterance to pray how he did because he had no formal education.

My grandmother served as a missionary in the missionary circle. My sister and I sang in the children's choir and also served as junior ushers. Both of us received Christ as our personal savior at an early age. I was baptized at age 11 and my sister at age 12.

Faith in Christ was always paramount in my life. I remained faithful in the ministries of my church until I relocated to New York in 1974. My spiritual roots and foundation today are a result of the teachings I received in the South during my early years as a child and as a young adult.

As I fast forward into young adulthood, I am reminded of what King David wrote in Psalm 139:13, *"God, you created my inmost being, you knit me together in my mother's womb."* Psalm 139:16 says, *"All the days ordained for me were written in your book before one of them came to be."* God knew me before my mother and my father ever got together. I was pre-ordained to be here before the foundation of the world.

eleven

BREAKING FREE FROM THE NEGATIVE PAST

How can I not think back to the life that my mother endured and wonder if my life would be different or if my life would take the same path as hers? But none of this changes my value in the eyes of God. He loves me anyway. I am still the apple of His eye and His prized possession.

From what I know now, one of the first steps to overcoming generational dysfunction is to recognize what you are dealing with and not to ignore it. I want to start a new pattern of goodness and love for my family. I can choose to change and set a new standard because God has given all of us a free will to make decisions. Every right choice I make can overturn the wrong patterns that other people in my family lineage have made.

Sadly, hurting people often end up hurting other people. You hear people say, *"I'm never going to raise my children the way I was raised."* The truth is, more often than not, they end up doing exactly what they said they would never do. That spirit is passed down and some day it will show up.

I remember being a single parent raising my oldest son. Whenever I verbally reprimanded him, I found myself using the same tone of voice that my grandfather used when he reprimanded me as a child. He would speak to me in a tone that put total fear in me. There was never a need to pursue any other method of discipline because I would become an emotional wreck with big *alligator tears* streaming down my face.

When my grandfather saw or realized how fearful I was, his tone would change to a softer, more calming voice. I saw my son react to me in the same manner. Looking at his face and watching the tears stream down the same way mine had done, brought me back to the reality that I needed to change. It was unacceptable to use the excuse, "that's the way I was spoken to as a child."

Thank God you and I can do something about our actions. Scripture says in Ephesians 6:12, *"We fight not against flesh and blood, but we fight in the spiritual realm."* I knew I had a responsibility to take authority over my behavior. I decided that I was not going to live that way any longer. I knew that God would give me the power to do what I needed to do to break this behavior. I didn't want to play the blame game. I had to take responsibility for my actions.

Even with good intentions, your past has a way of resurfacing at some point in your life. Even in adulthood, life can knock you down in a way that you don't expect. One of my hardest experiences was enduring a three-year marriage of severe domestic violence by a chemically dependent spouse. The marriage ended in divorce, and I became a single parent raising a young child alone, working two jobs to support both of us. I was also attending college full-time to obtain a degree, not only to fulfill my dreams, but to improve the quality of life for myself and my son.

Yes, I have experienced some unfair things in the past that have made life more difficult for me. But, after years of prayer and seeing the blessings of God upon my life, my attitude is, *"I am not going to sit around moaning and complaining about how I was raised or how somebody mistreated me. This is the life God gave me and I have a responsibility to make the most of it."* It's a personal decision to make good choices every day. As I do this, I believe God will put a stop to any negative patterns that may have been a part of my family bloodline for so many years. I can be the one to make a difference.

God planned everything and arranged for me to be here at this particular time in history. It is through His grace that I was able to come to the realization and embrace the fact that I do have destiny and value. God has helped me to understand that my value is not based on how unsuccessful I may think I am or on how somebody else has treated me. My value is based solely on the fact that I am a child of the Most High God even with all of my mistakes and weaknesses.

God is merciful. In every hardship meant for evil, He brought good out of it. He blessed me with a godly husband who loves the Lord and who is the wonderful father of our children. I praise God for our 25 years of marriage.

He has blessed me with a formal education to obtain undergraduate and graduate degrees including a Master's in Christian Counseling and a Doctorate of Ministry in Christian Theology. He has elevated me as an ordained minister, currently serving on the ministerial staff at Westbury Gospel Tabernacle, my church of 20 years.

God, in His favor, has placed me in the position of Director of The Leeds Place North Shore Children and Family Guidance Center, where I have been employed for 25 years.

I don't always understand how I made it this far, but I do know that without God I would not have made it at all. I still face many struggles: fear of rejection, low self-esteem, and a negative self-image. But I do know that God remains faithful and continues to open doors for me. I have no idea what tomorrow may bring, but I do know the One who created my tomorrow and I trust Him.

I know that the decisions I make today will affect my children, my grandchildren and generations to come. Therefore, I don't want to leave any wrong attitudes or mindsets that could potentially be passed down to the next generation to struggle with. It is my desire to leave my family better off than they were before. I don't want bad habits, selfishness, bad choices, prejudice and unforgiveness to diminish my life. I want everything about my life now to make it easier on those who will come after me.

I want to pass down good qualities: integrity, compassion, and godliness. Every day that I stay faithful and overcome another obstacle, I am storing up equity and blessings for future generations. My dreams may not come to pass exactly as I would have hoped, but I believe that the seeds I have sown will be harvested by my sons and my grandchildren.

The Scripture says in I Chronicles 4:40 that God's people left the place where they lived better off than it was when they found it, *"and they found rich, good pasture, and the land was spacious, quiet, and peaceful."* This is my personal goal: to leave my family more joy, more faith, more favor, and more victory.

I was not raised by my biological parents but I was certainly blessed by everything that was handed down by my maternal grandparents, regardless of the manner in which it came. God always miraculously turned it around for my good.

I know that I am where I am today because somebody in my family prayed for me. Somebody took a stand for righteousness. Somebody stuck with his (or her) commitment. Somebody lived a life of integrity. My forefathers, most of whom I never met, planted good seeds in my life.

Living a life of integrity and excellence that honors God is worth more to me than all the material possessions that may be part of the legacy to my children. To pass on the favor and blessings of God to my future generations is worth more than anything else in this world.

I AM MY MOTHER'S DAUGHTER

SEVEN POINTS OF HEALING
Mind, Body and Spirit

1. Have a grateful attitude; stay positive no matter what the circumstance. Find the good in every situation.

2. Exercise your faith in God. Expect God's best for your life. Take action to fill your life with healthy activities while eliminating any unhealthy actions, attitudes or lifestyle issues.

3. Do not let others set limits for you. Reach for something beyond where you are now. Actively pursue new goals and expect to meet them all.

4. Make the best better. Look for ways to improve your life. Choose to be kind, gentle and loving toward all people.

5. Actively pursue a deeper relationship with God. Establish a daily time for prayer, praise, meditation and worship.

6. Learn to accept who you are. You are God's original design because you are made in His likeness.

7. Live life as a positive reflection of who God is. Put action behind your faith and leave a lasting legacy for your family and the world.

You have not seen, heard or imagined the great things God has in store for you. As you continue striving to reach that next level; improving your life and reaching for your highest potential, you will not only give birth to your dreams, but you will become better than you ever dreamed possible.

"Set your goals beyond your reach and you will always have something to strive for." - MOTTO: GC SHAW HIGH SCHOOL - CLASS OF 1968

REFLECTIONS

As a society, we are not always moved to help someone else who is hurting. Sometimes our expectation is for them to move into the "get over it" stage. But, we cannot rush people through their pain. We cannot judge where they are emotionally or push them back into a state of normalcy.

Pain is the number one experience most of us would love to live without. It is often the pain of tragic circumstances and life issues that cause us to be pushed to our limit. All of us respond in different ways and should never underestimate someone else's pain. While their hurt and disappointment may seem far less than what we have experienced, the results are no less devastating. Pain is pain.

Suffering people are often overlooked. The deep internal pain they carry can become a breeding ground for depression, frustration, anger, loneliness, physical illness and even death. However, God is aware of everything we face in our lives and understands the purpose for which it happens.

If we would close our eyes and take a moment to hear what God is saying to us, we would understand that He is not trying to destroy us. He is working out His purpose for our lives. He is well aware of how to utilize the pain of the past to help us walk toward our destiny. He wants us to do what His Word says, *"Cast all your anxiety on Him because He cares for you."* I Peter 5:7.

Since I have given my life to Christ and committed myself to the call of ministry, I have often wondered whether I am worthy of such a call. As I think about it, I know that ministering the Word of God to people – whether to one person or ten thousand – is something I want to do for the rest of my life. It's a blessing to hear from God and a privilege to encourage someone else with His word.

"I thank Christ Jesus our Lord, who has given me strength, that He considered me faithful, appointing me to His service." I Timothy 1:12.

When I accepted my call to ministry, it was as though a burden had been lifted from my heart. Even not knowing why God had chosen me, I was ready and willing to trust Him for everything I lacked, beginning with my self-confidence and self-worth. God predestined and chose me. He created me. He had a pattern for my life; the woman He called me to be, and the purpose He wanted to fulfill through me.

"For those God foreknew He also predestined to be conformed to the likeness of His Son, that He might be the firstborn among many brothers. And those He predestined, He also called, those He called He also justified, those He justified, He also glorified." Romans 8:29-30.

Life has been pre-ordained by God. He foreknew everything that would take place and planned His purpose accordingly. God knows what we can handle even when we don't believe we can. He allows the firestorms of life to come our way because He knows that with His help we can handle the heat. God rewards us with blessings of joy, peace, love and prosperity in the midst of the storm because He wants to give us His best.

Remember that if God established a plan for your life before challenges occurred, then He will make provisions for you to endure them. God sees your heart. He knows the tears you would shed and the anger and hurt you would feel. Trust Him and His word, especially in the difficult seasons of your life. The answers to all of your questions are established in His word. Follow His voice and He will direct your path.

No matter what twists and turns life brings, you can find the good if you look for it. If you have the right attitude, you can see the sun shining even when it's cloudy. You can stay full of joy even when things around you don't go your way.

In this season of your life, you may be experiencing or have experienced something that is hindering your ability to fulfill the purpose God has ordained for you. I would ask that you take a moment to evaluate where you are by responding to these questions. Your responses will help you to know and understand the purpose that God has established for you:

- Am I aware of the purpose God has for my life?
- Will I trust God to know and plan my future?
- Is God working in me to achieve the greater good?
- Will I use my experiences and struggles to minister effectively to someone else?

I believe there is a void in every person that only a relationship with God can fill. Knowing His Son, the Lord Jesus Christ is the only source of true peace and fulfillment in life. My prayer is that God will give us a spirit of gratitude so that we will always focus on the good and never take life for granted. If you will trust God each day and live according to His plan for your life, you will be happier, healthier, and you will rise higher than you ever imagined possible. You have seeds of greatness in you. Rise out of complacency, keep growing, keep reaching higher heights. Your best days are still ahead of you.

I AM MY MOTHER'S DAUGHTER

RESOURCES

What is Maternal Depression?

It is estimated that one in ten pregnant women and 13% of new mothers experience depression. Maternal depression is a mood disorder that begins before or immediately after childbirth. It affects a mother's ability to adequately care for her young child. This inability to meet a child's basic needs can lead to long-term, adverse effects on the child's health and well-being.

SAFETY

Mothers who suffer from maternal depression are less likely to implement safety measures in the home such as the use of safety gates and electrical outlet covers, or car seats in their vehicles. Babies with depressed mothers are less likely to have routines in place, such as established eating and sleeping habits. Mothers can become suicidal and even homicidal towards their infant.

SYMPTOMS

Early detection of maternal depression can be difficult to diagnose, as a lot of pregnancy and depression symptoms are the same. Some of these symptoms include fatigue, crying, hopelessness, anxiety, problems concentrating, changes in appetite, sleeping difficulty and lack of interest in daily activities.

Baby Blues

Eight percent of new mothers experience the "baby blues," but this is not maternal depression. These conditions have some of the same symptoms, but the "baby blues" normally go away after a couple of weeks. Maternal depression lasts much longer.

Treatment

Treatment for maternal depression can include a combination of psychotherapy and medication. Change in lifestyle such as getting enough rest, reducing stress, increasing exercise and eating a healthy diet can also help manage symptoms of maternal depression.

Resource/Reference: New York State Department of Health

What is Postpartum Depression?

Postpartum depression is moderate to severe depression in a woman after she has given birth. It may occur soon after delivery or up to a year later. Most of the time, it occurs within the first three months after delivery.

Symptoms

Feelings of anxiety, irritability, tearfulness, and restlessness are common in the week or two after pregnancy. These symptoms almost always go away soon without the need for treatment.

Postpartum depression may occur when the "baby blues" do not fade away or when signs of depression start one or more months after childbirth. A mother with postpartum depression may have negative feelings toward the baby or even think about harming the baby.

The symptoms of postpartum depression are the same as the symptoms of depression that occur at other times in life.

Treatment

A new mother who has any symptoms of postpartum depression should contact her doctor or nurse right away to get help. The treatment of depression after childbirth often includes medication, therapy, or both. Support groups may be helpful, but they should not replace medication or professional talk therapy if you have been diagnosed with postpartum depression.

Resource/Reference: Public Medical Health

captured
MOMENTS

MARTHA HAYES TAYLOR
*1898-1868. My Maternal
Step-Grandmother*

OLIVIA TAYLOR, MARROW, DANIELS
AGE 21. *1918-1953.
My Beloved Mother*

MR. JOHN HENRY TAYLOR, JR.
*1887-1976. My Maternal
Grandfather (far left) celebrating
a birthday with a family friend.*

captured
MOMENTS

MRS. LUCINDA L. POOLE
My most inspirational teacher and mentor.
"Long will I remember those ideals
which you have strived so hard to instill
withiin me. Your inspiration and the
knowledge I have gained will always
be before me, guiding me toward my
goals and objectives of life."

MRS. MARIE DOWNEY
My Godmother

ISBN 978-0-692-58789-8

28150933R00049

Made in the USA
San Bernardino, CA
21 December 2015